The Secret

by Julie Haydon

illustrated by Kiera Poelsma

OXFORD
UNIVERSITY PRESS
AUSTRALIA & NEW ZEALAND

Last Saturday morning,
Tess and her mum were walking
past Alex's house.
They saw Alex's mum at her car.

"Hi," said Tess.

3

Alex's mum jumped.

"I didn't see you there, Tess," she said.

"Alex isn't home.
He's out with his dad."

Tess saw a shiny red bike
in the back of the car.
"Is that bike for Alex's birthday?"
she asked.

6

"Yes," said Alex's mum.

"But it's a secret, Tess. You can't tell Alex."

"I won't tell Alex," said Tess.
"I can keep a secret."

All week, Alex talked about his birthday.

Tess wanted to tell him about the shiny red bike. But it was a secret!

11

The next Saturday, Alex had a birthday party at his house.

He raced up to Tess. "Come and look at what I got!" he said.

13

Alex showed off his new bike.

Alex's mum came and stood next to Tess. "Thanks for keeping the secret, Tess," she said.

Tess smiled.

"I *can* keep a secret."

Endangered Australian Animals

by Carmel Reilly

Contents

OXFORD
UNIVERSITY PRESS
AUSTRALIA & NEW ZEALAND

Endangered Animals

Endangered animals are animals that are in danger of dying out.

Animals can become endangered because of threats from:

- hunting
- changes to their habitat
- pollution.

Wester
Austral

western swamp turtle

pygmy

er shark

northern hairy-nosed wombat

Northern
Territory

Queensland

South
Australia

New South
Wales

giant dragonfly

Victoria

Australian
Capital
Territory

Tasmania

orange-bellied parrot

gue lizard

3

Northern Hairy-nosed Wombat

This is a northern hairy-nosed wombat.

These animals used to live in Queensland, New South Wales and Victoria. Now there are only a few hundred of them left in Queensland.

●	**LEGEND**
	northern hairy-nosed wombats live here

Queensland

Habitat

woodland

Diet

grass

Threats

loss of habitat from farming

dogs

Orange-bellied Parrot

This is an orange-bellied parrot.

These birds lived in New South Wales, Victoria, South Australia and Tasmania. Now there are fewer than 90 adult birds left.

South Australia

New South Wales

Victoria

Tasmania

LEGEND

● orange-bellied parrots live here

Habitat

salt marshes

Diet

grass and seeds

Threats

loss of habitat from farming

cats

foxes

Western Swamp Turtle

This is a western swamp turtle.

Thousands of these turtles lived in swamplands along the west coast of Australia. Now, there are only about 100 left.

Western Australia

LEGEND

● western swamp turtles live here

Habitat

swampland

Diet

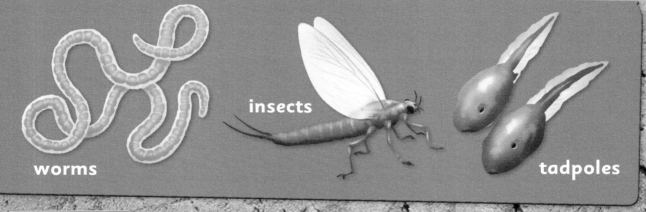

worms

insects

tadpoles

Threats

loss of habitat from farming

cats

dogs

foxes

9

Northern River Shark

This is a northern river shark.

These animals lived in the oceans to the north of Australia. Now, there are fewer than 250 adult sharks left.

Australia

LEGEND
- northern river sharks live here

Habitat

river mouths and bays

Diet

fish

Threats

fishing

Giant Dragonfly

This is a
giant dragonfly.

These dragonflies
lived around swamps
along the coast of New South Wales.
Now, there are only a few places
where they live.

New South Wales

LEGEND
● giant dragonflies live here

Habitat

swampland

Diet

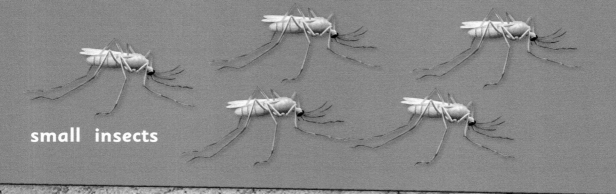

small insects

Threats

loss of habitat from farming

loss of habitat from pollution

13

Pygmy Blue-tongue Lizard

This is a pygmy blue-tongue lizard.

These lizards lived in a large area around Adelaide. Now, there are only a few thousand left.

South Australia

LEGEND
● pygmy blue-tongue lizards live here

Habitat

scrubland

Diet

insects

Threats

loss of habitat from farming

15

These Australian animals are in danger of dying out. They are endangered animals.

orange-bellied parrot

pygmy blue-tongue lizard

western swamp turtle

northern hairy-nosed wombat

northern river shark

giant dragonfly